MARRIAGE ^{Rx}

10

PRESCRIPTIONS
FOR A HAPPY
MARRIAGE

WORKBOOK &
STUDY GUIDE

PASTOR (MRS.) MODUPE SANUSI

Published by
Eleviv Strategy Group

MARRIAGE RX - 10 PRESCRIPTIONS FOR A HAPPY MARRIAGE
WORKBOOK & STUDY GUIDE
(FOR NEWLYWEDS, ENGAGED & MARRIED COUPLES)

COPYRIGHT © 2011 BY PASTOR (MRS.) MODUPE SANUSI
PUBLISHED BY ELEVIV STRATEGY GROUP
HOUSTON, TEXAS 77082

Unless otherwise indicated all Scriptures marked KJV are taken from the King James Version.

Cover Design by www.thinkingmen.net
Interior Design by www.Adonaigroupinc.net

1. Inspirational 2. Relationships 3. Marriage

ISBN 978-1-935653-12-7

Printed and bound in the USA
10 9 8 7 6 5 4 3 2 1

Table of Contents

DEDICATION

This book is dedicated to my Lord and Savior, Jesus Christ, who led me to my darling husband.

It is secondarily dedicated to my husband who, by His grace, is a child of God and gave me a clear picture of what true love and Christian marriage should be.

Introduction

This workbook is written with you and your spouse in mind; it is a masterpiece that will help each of you put into practice the things you have learned. I encourage husbands and wives to, thoughtfully, go through the couples project and study the Word of God together as they journey through the pages of this study guide.

This is a great tool for newlyweds, engaged couples and seasoned married couples, who are willing to give their marriages a jump-start. In order to benefit from this workbook, I recommend you study, individually, and then come together to discuss key issues that affect your marriage. The romantic ideas can be used for date ideas, and so much more, as you learn how to love again and reignite your relationship. I also encourage each of you to answer the questions truthfully and be open to learn more about yourself and your spouse in the process. Make sure you apply as much as you can to your marital life and you will be amazed at how much it will transform your home.

The workbook does not promise to change you, or your spouse, overnight; rather, as both of you apply the simple practices recommended in the lessons, each attempt will, little by little, help transform your mind and change your marriage. The study guide is designed to take you beyond mere intellectual understanding to the point where the ideas of this book take you over and dominate your way of thinking and ultimately change your marriage.

Couples Commitment Certificate

This is to certify that I,

_____

promise to work through this study with you,

_____

I promise to keep an open-mind as we learn together, and

build up a better, enduring, and godly relationship.

Signature   Date

_____   _____

Signature   Date

_____   _____

_____

TO MY WIFE

This is to certify that I,

_____

have read and understood what it means to love

you and how loving you is my calling and a

mandate from above.

I promise to do all that is possible to show you how

much I want us to have a happy home and how

much you mean to me.

Signature   Date

_____   _____

TO MY HUSBAND

This is to certify that I,

_____

have read and understood what it means to love

you and how loving you is my calling and

a mandate from above.

I promise to do all that is possible to show you how

much I want us to have a happy home and how

much you mean to me.

Signature   Date

_____   _____

Couples Project 1
God and your Marriage

Building an Altar in Your Home

For where two or three are gathered together in my name, there am I in the midst of them. Matthew 18:20 (King James Version)

Marriage Check-Up

1. What can a family altar do for your marriage?

   _____

   _____

   _____

   _____

2. Is God the head of your home? _____

   _____

   _____

   _____

   _____

3. Do you recognize His authority in your marriage?

   _____

   _____

4. How is your spiritual life on a scale of 1 to 10, (10 being the best).

   1   2   3   4   5   6   7   8   9   10

5. How is your spouse's spiritual life on a scale of 1 to 10, (10 being the best).

   1   2   3   4   5   6   7   8   9   10

6. What areas are you struggling with as a couple?

   _____

   _____

   _____

   _____

7. What areas are both of you struggling with, individually?

   _____

   _____

   _____

   _____

8. What areas of your marriage haven't you surrendered to God completely?

   _____

   _____

   _____

   _____

9. Do you listen to God? YES or NO_____ How?

_____

_____

_____

_____

10. Do you struggle with praying and fasting over issues in your marriage?

_____

_____

_____

_____

11. How often do you pray for your spouse?

_____

_____

12. How often do you pray for your children?

_____

_____

13. How often do you pray for extended family? (Yours and our spouse's)

_____

_____

    How often do you pray together as a family?
        Daily____ Once a Week____ Twice a Week____

14. Are you helping to build your spouse's spiritual life?
    YES or NO _____ How? _____

_____

_____

How do you plan to do better?

_____

_____

_____

15. How are you showing forth the love of Christ through your marriage?

_____

_____

_____

_____

PRAYER

Lord, help us to put you first in our family and in our marriage, give us the strength to lead this family in the way of the Lord. Help us to love each other and let your love show forth through our marriage. Reveal to us the purpose of our marriage and give us the strength to walk in it.

Reflections for Him

_____

_____

_____

_____

_____

_____

_____

_____

_____

_____

Reflections for Her

_____

_____

_____

_____

_____

_____

_____

_____

_____

Notes

Love and Your Marriage

Love has a lot to do with it

And now abideth faith, hope, charity, these three; but the greatest of these is charity. 1 Corinthians 13:13 (King James Version)

Loving your spouse is an important step in having a happy marriage. Showing your love for your spouse everyday makes for a happy marriage; It's not about the big things, but the little things you can do to show forth Gods love in the most profound and effective way. Loving your spouse is not a choice; it is a mandate from God.

Marriage Check-Up

1. Do you love your spouse?

   _____

   _____

2. Has the intensity of your love diminished overtime? YES or NO

   Why?_____

   _____

   _____

   _____

3. How might you reignite your love for your spouse?

   _____

_____

_____

_____

4. How often do you say I love you?

_____

_____

_____

_____

5. Do you have pet names for each other?

_____

_____

What are they?

_____

_____

6. How do you show your spouse you love him/her?

_____

_____

_____

7. Do you know the purpose of your marriage?

_____

_____

_____

8. What is your definition of love?

_____

_____

_____

_____

9. If God so loved the world, that He gave ----, how does this translate into your marriage relationship?

_____

_____

_____

_____

10. Is it possible to love, the unlovable? YES or NO_____

Why?_____

_____

_____

_____

PRAYER

Lord, I pray that you heal my heart of all loneliness. Lord, teach me how to love my spouse the way you loved the Church and gave your Son for it. Teach me how to love no matter what.

Reflections for Him

_____

_____

_____

_____

_____

_____

_____

_____

_____

_____

_____

Reflections for Her

_____

_____

_____

_____

_____

_____

_____

_____

_____

_____

_____

Notes

SEX IN MARRIAGE
Keeping Your Marriage Exciting

[3]Let the husband render unto the wife due benevolence: and likewise also the wife unto the husband.

[4]The wife hath not power of her own body, but the husband: and likewise also the husband hath not power of his own body, but the wife.

[5]Defraud ye not one the other, except it be with consent for a time, that ye may give yourselves to fasting and prayer; and come together again, that Satan tempt you not for your incontinency.
1 Corinthians 7:3-5 (King James Version)

Marriage Check-Up

1. Grade your sex life 5 being the best, 1 being the worst, and 0 being a non-existent sex life.

0	1	2	3	4	5
Nothing	I just enjoy the ride	I'd rather be shopping	On and Off	Can't Complain	Amazing

2. Do you pray about your sex life? YES or NO_____

_____

_____

3. What are your views about sex?

_____

_____

_____

_____

4. Who or what shaped your attitude towards sex?

_____

_____

_____

How has that affected your sex life with your spouse?

_____

_____

_____

5. To me, sex is?
   a. Dirty and shouldn't be talked about.
   b. Okay as long as we both don't talk about it.
   c. Just for procreation, no need for all that stuff.
   d. A special gift from God.
   e. A way to show my spouse how much I love him/her.
   f. One of the only ways I can show how much I love him/her.

6. How often do you spend time together?

_____

_____

_____

7. How often do you have sex? (Circle One)
   a. Daily   Weekly
   b. Once a Month

c. Once a year

d. Can't remember the last time

e. Only when it's time to make a baby

8. Do you think motherhood should negatively impact your sex life?

1	2	3	4	5
Strongly disagree	disagree	neutral	agree	strongly agree

9. If I rated the importance of sex to me in this marriage (on a scale of 1-the lowest to 10-the highest), my score would be

_____

10. What I'm most concerned about in our sex life or potential

sex life is:_____

_____

11. *The way(s) I like to prepare* for sex is:

_____

_____

_____

12. I wish I could tell my spouse the things I like him/her to do when we are making love:

_____

_____

_____

13. Foreplay to me means:

_____

_____

_____

14. A personal problem I've had in my sex life is:

_____

_____

_____

How that problem has or might impact our sex life is:

_____

_____

_____

15. If there are problems in our sex life, the way(s) I would like for us to address it would be to:

_____

_____

_____

_____

_____

PRAYER

Lord, I pray that you heal our sex life. Lord, help us to learn how to be passionate and show love in this very special way. Preserve our marriage; help us not to defile our marriage bed. Help us to be free with one other, and communicate issues in our sex life that hinder our happiness in this marriage. Lord, teach me how to love my spouse the way you loved the Church and gave your Son for it.

Reflections for Him

_____

_____

_____

_____

_____

_____

_____

_____

_____

Reflections for Her

_____

_____

_____

_____

_____

_____

_____

_____

_____

Couples Project 2
Finance in Marriage

For wisdom is a defence, and money is a defence: but the excellency of knowledge is, that wisdom giveth life to them that have it. Ecclesiastes 7:12 (King James Version)

Marriage Check-Up

Rate yourself and your spouse on the following two statements:

a. I pay my tithes faithfully, I understand that what I have is of God and I am only a steward.

Poorly reflect   Strongly reflect

1   2   3   4   5   6   7   8   9   10

Why?

_____

_____

_____

_____

_____

b. My spouse pays his or her tithes faithfully, he/she understands that what he/she has is of God and that he/she is only a steward.

Poorly reflect   Strongly reflect

| 1 | 2 | 3 | 4 | 5 | 6 | 7 | 8 | 9 | 10 |

Why?

_____

_____

_____

Individually, make a list of at least ten material possessions you highly value. Then share your list with each other.

1._____

2._____

3._____

4._____

5._____

6._____

7._____

8._____

9._____

10. _____

1. What money means to me is:

_____

_____

_____

_____

2. Saving money for us has been hard/easy because:

_____

_____

_____

_____

3. Do you keep money secrets? YES or NO_____

   Why?_____

   _____

   _____

4. Do you have an emergency fund? YES or NO_____

5. Do you consult with your spouse before making big purchases or making an investment? YES or NO_____

6. Do you have a hush, hush account your spouse knows nothing about? YES or NO_____

7. We live beyond our means. YES or NO _____

8. Who is the spender? _____Who is the saver? _____
   (You or Your spouse)

9. My current total amount of debt is $_____

10. My current credit score is _____which I consider to be _____
    poor; _____ average; _____ excellent.

11. My current salary is $_____

12. Is God at the center of your finances? YES or NO _____

13. Do you pay your tithes and offering? YES or NO _____

14. Do you give to the poor and needy?   YES or NO _____

15. Joint account or Not? _____ Why?_____

_____

_____

_____

Do you both know where important documents, such as insurance documents, wills, tax information, bank account numbers, investment information, etc. are located? YES or NO (Circle One) Why?

_____

_____

_____

How much do the two of you owe in debts and what are your assets?

_____

_____

_____

Budget

Where does your money go? Do you have a workable budget?

_____

_____

_____

Financial Planning

Do you both have any financial goals for your future?
Short-term Goals:

_____

_____

_____

Long-term Goals:

_____

_____

_____

Financial Vulnerability

Where are the two of you most vulnerable in your finances?

    a. Lack of job security
    b. Over spending
    c. Insufficient income
    d. Too much debt
    e. Investments

Decide together how to strengthen your financial position. (Write down steps to take individually and as a couple):

_____

_____

_____

_____

_____

Bill Paying

Who pays the bills? _____

Do you do this together as a couple or has one of you volunteered for this task? Reevaluate if the way you have this set up is working or not.

Financial Differences

Do you think your upbringing influences the way you view money?

YES or NO _____ Why?_____

_____

_____

_____

_____

How much income would you like to make (together) this next year?

    a. $0.00-5,000
    b. $5,000-10,000
    c. $10,000-50,000
    d. $50,000-100,000
    e. $100,000-$500,000
    f. $500,000-1,000,000
    g. $1,000,000 and up

How much extra income would you like to make (together) this next year?

    a. $0.00-5,000
    b. $5,000-10,000
    c. $10,000-50,000
    d. $50,000-100,000
    e. $100,000-$500,000
    f. $500,000-1,000,000
    g. $1,000,000 and up

How long do you expect both of you to continue working outside the home?

    a.   1year-5years
    b.   5years-10years
    c.   10years-20years
    d.   20years-30years
    e.   30years-40years
    f.   40years and up

What do you think about credit cards?

   a. I love them-can't live without them
   b. They are for emergencies only
   c. I can't stand them

How many credit cards do you have now? _____

How much do you owe on each?

_____ _____

_____ _____

_____ _____

_____ _____

_____ _____

Is your family income supporting your standard of living? YES or
NO _____ Why?_____

_____

_____

Do you think children should be given an allowance? If so, how
much at ages five, ten, fifteen, twenty-one? If not, why not?

_____

_____

How do you feel about borrowing money from your parents, friends,
or relatives?_____

_____

_____

How do you feel about sending money to relatives in other countries?

_____

_____

_____

How much is reasonable to send? Weekly _____ Monthly _____ Quarterly _____ Yearly_____

How do you feel about loaning money to friends or relatives? What if they couldn't pay it back?

_____

_____

_____

What percent of our income would we be saving? _____

How often should we save? Weekly _____ Bi-weekly _____ Monthly _____

How much should we spend on special occasions like:

- Birthdays: each other's parents, children, friends, others_____
- Anniversaries: our own, parents, friends, relatives, others_____
- Other special days: Mother's Day, Father's Day, Valentine's Day_____
- Christmas: each other's gifts, parents, children, other relatives, coworkers, friends, Christmas tree, decorations

_____

_____

- Baby showers, bridal showers, weddings, etc.

_____

_____

Who should do the gift buying for birthdays? Anniversaries? Christmas? Other special days?

_____

_____

What should be the dollar limit on purchases made without the other person's knowledge? Why?

_____

_____

What are your feelings about a monthly budget?

_____

_____

What are your feelings about a will?

_____

_____

What should the children inherit when we die?

_____

_____

What investments do you have today?

_____

_____

_____

PRAYER

Lord, we place our finances in your care, please help us to learn how to spend wisely, give wisely and save more. Lord, help us to be faithful tithers and teach us how to give to those that are less fortunate. Help us to keep an open line of communication when it comes to money. Lord, give us the power to make wealth. In Jesus name, Amen.

Reflections for Him

_____
_____
_____
_____
_____
_____
_____
_____
_____
_____

Reflections for Her

_____
_____
_____
_____
_____
_____
_____
_____
_____
_____

Monthly Income / Expense Record

Expense	Due Date	Present Amount	Projected Future Amt
Rent/Mortgage			
Gas/Oil			
Electric			
Water/Sewage			
Phone			
Life Insurance			
Car Insurance			
Taxes (if not included in mortgage)			
Homeowner's/Tenant Insurance (if not included in mortgage)			
Installment loan with _____			
Installment loan with _____			
Charge Account _____			
Charge Account _____			
Charge Account _____			
Charge Account _____			
Charge Account _____			
Food-Grocery Store			
Auto expenses			
Gasoline/Transportation			
Medical (doctor, dentist, eye care, prescriptions)			
Daycare			
Lunches/snacks, coffee, etc.			
Cable TV			
Pay per view, video rental			
Dry cleaning, laundry			
Education expenses (including books)			
Church/religious donations			
Other donations			
Pet expenses			
Barber/hair salon			
Allowances (including children)			
Entertainment			
Newspaper/magazines, etc.			
Babysitting expenses			
Fast Food			
Clubs, sports hobbies			
New clothing/shoes			
College Funds			
Gifts-Birthdays, anniversaries			

Gifts-Holidays			
Emergency Savings			
Saving for _____			
Other Expenses			

_____ - _____ = $ _____

Total Net Income   **Total Expenses**

Monthly Income		**Monthly Expenses**	
Your Pay	$	Rent or Mortgage	$
Spouse's Pay	$	Utilities (Phone, gas, electric, cable, etc.)	$
Bonuses	$	Insurance (home, auto, life, health, etc.)	$
Commissions	$	Food	$
Tips	$	Incidental Home (paper products, non-food items, etc.)	$
Interest Received	$	Clothing	$
Investment Earnings	$	Auto (gas, tolls, maintenance)	$
Rental Income	$	Debt Payments (auto, credit cards, store cards, etc.)	$
Pension Income	$	Child Care	$
Social Security Income	$	Health (medical, dental, eye, etc./not covered by insurance)	$
Alimony Received	$	Taxes (not taken out of paycheck)	$
Other Income	$	Gifts (charities, church, holidays, birthdays, etc.)	$
	$	Entertainment (movies, vacation, videos, etc.)	$
	$	Personal Allowances	$
	$	Other Expenses	$
Totals	$		$

Children and Marriage

Let No Child Put Asunder

"Lo, children are an heritage of the Lord: and the fruit of the womb is his reward." Psalm 127:3 (King James Version)

Marriage Check-Up

1. Do you put your children before your spouse? YES or NO _____

   Why?_____

   _____

   _____

2. Who has the responsibility of training your children?
   Why?_____

   _____

   _____

3. When was the last time you both went out or took some time out to be alone with each other?

   _____

   _____

   _____

4. Have you made your children a sort of distraction in your marriage? YES or NO_____ Why? _____

_____

_____

_____

_____

5. Do you resent your spouse for neglecting you and focusing on the children? YES or NO_____ Why? _____

_____

_____

_____

_____

6. How has that affected your love life with your spouse?

_____

_____

_____

(Talk about how you plan to raise your children)

7. Whose responsibility is it to train the children? _____

8. What are your expectations for your children? _____

_____

_____

9. Do you involve your teenage children in decision making at home? YES or NO _____ Why or why not? _____

_____

_____

_____

10. List what type of children you plan to have/or already have: (Godly Children, Intelligent, Articulate, Creative, etc.)

_____

_____

_____

Learn to nurture the gifts and talents your children have, know that God is the giver of good gifts. So nurture it.

11. What discipline style do you use with your children?

_____

_____

_____

12. What discipline style does your spouse use?

_____

_____

_____

13. Can your children see the love of Christ in your home?

_____

_____

_____

GOING THROUGH A SEASON OF PURPOSE

1. How has the period of infertility affected your marriage?

_____

_____

2. What influence do your in-laws have over the issue?

_____

_____

_____

_____

_____

3. Have you tried following the wrong counsel or alternative ways to solve the problem? What and why?

_____

_____

_____

_____

_____

4. Are you both seeking God daily regarding the issue?

_____

_____

_____

_____

_____

_____

5. Do you feel inadequate about your season of infertility?
   Why?_____

   _____

   _____

   _____

6. Is your spouse willing to seek medical help to find out if there are health issues to consider?

   _____

   _____

   _____

Remember God has the final say in your life and marriage, He only is the giver of good gifts and will give you your heart's desire. Keep trusting in Him.

PRAYER

Father, help us to recognize the blessings you have given us. We thank you for the godly children you gave us, help us to train them in the way of the Lord, and help us to know that our marriage is still a focal point in our home. Help us to love each other and also have enough love to share with the children you have blessed us with. Strengthen our family and let our family be a source of inspiration to others.

GOING THROUGH A SEASON OF PURPOSE

PRAYER

Lord we thank you for this season of purpose, Lord teach us what you want us to learn at this time as we wait on you for the fruit of the womb. We thank you because your Word said none shall be barren in the land, and that children are an heritage of the Lord: and the fruit of the womb is his reward. Lord, bless us with this gift, at your appointed time, and help us not to grow weary. Heal us from bitterness and anger and help us not to listen to ungodly counsel at this time. Lord, strengthen us and keep us together as we draw closer to you.

Reflections for Him

_____

_____

_____

_____

_____

_____

_____

_____

Reflections for Her

Communication and Your Marriage

Speak It Out!

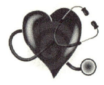

A good man out of the good treasure of his heart bringeth forth that which is good; and an evil man out of the evil treasure of his heart bringeth forth that which is evil: for of the abundance of the heart his mouth speaketh. Luke 6:45 (King James Version)

Marriage Check-Up

1. How do you feel you can begin communicating better than you already are?

   _____

   _____

   _____

2. Do you always have to be right? YES or NO _____

   Why?_____

   _____

   _____

3. Do you feel that there is anything keeping either one, or both of you, from sharing your feelings and communicating effectively?

_____

_____

_____

_____

4. What should be your part in freeing your marriage from those restraints?

_____

_____

_____

_____

5. Do you listen effectively?

_____

_____

_____

_____

6. Does your spouse listen to you when you talk?

_____

_____

_____

_____

7. Do you avoid confrontation?

_____

_____

_____

_____

8. How do you react when you get angry?

_____

_____

_____

_____

9. Do you settle it first on your knees?

_____

_____

_____

_____

10. Are you a nag?

_____

_____

11. Is your spouse a nag?

_____

_____

12. Are you a selective listener?

_____

_____

_____

_____

13. List a few attitudes you would like to change:

_____

_____

_____

14. List areas you think your spouse can fix in his or her attitude?

_____

_____

_____

_____

15. These things ticks me off:

_____

_____

_____

_____

_____

16. I would appreciate it if my spouse quits saying this?

_____

_____

_____

_____

17. Do you have family meetings? YES or NO _____

    Why? Or, Why not? _____

    _____

    _____

    _____

    _____

18. How often do you sit and talk as a couple? Daily _____

    Weekly _____ Yearly _____ Never _____

    Sometimes _____ Why must we talk? _____

19. Do you avoid having conversations with your spouse so as to
    avoid conflict? YES or NO _____ Why? _____

    _____

    _____

    _____

    _____

20. Quiet? You _____, or Spouse _____

    Talkative? You _____, or Spouse _____ (Check One)

PRAYER

Lord, teach me to communicate effectively with my spouse, help me to learn how to listen as well. Teach me to bridle my tongue. Father, help me to settle my grievances on my knees first, before approaching my spouse. Help me not to be silent when I need to speak up, and teach me how to be patient with my spouse and not nitpick on everything he/she does.

Reflections for Him

_____
_____
_____
_____
_____
_____
_____
_____
_____

Reflections for Her

_____
_____
_____
_____
_____
_____
_____
_____
_____

Couples Project 3
Submission, Respect and
Your Marriage

Respect

"For this is how the holy women who hoped in God used to adorn themselves, by submitting to their own husbands, as Sarah obeyed Abraham, calling him lord. And you are her children, if you do good and do not fear anything that is frightening."
1 Peter 3:5-6(King James Version)

Marriage Check-Up

1. Is there anything you are doing or failing to do that seems to send a signal that you do not honor your husband or his leadership in your home?

    _____

    _____

    _____

    _____

2. Are you a tyrant in your home? YES or NO_____

3. Do you love your wife as Christ loved the church?
    YES or NO_____

4. Do you protect your wife's dignity? YES or NO_____

5. What does that mean?

_____

_____

_____

6. Do you feel as though, being independent excludes you from submitting to your husband? YES or NO _____ Why? _____

_____

_____

_____

7. Do you respect your spouse?-YES or NO _____ How?_____

_____

_____

_____

8. Do you feel like you are much smarter than your spouse and therefore should be the ultimate decision maker in your marriage? YES or NO _____ Explain_____

_____

_____

9. Do you feel because your spouse is not a believer, you have the right to undermine his authority?

_____

_____

_____

10. When you talk about your spouse to family and friends, how do you paint him/her?

_____

_____

11. Are you disrespectful? YES or NO _____

12. Are you rude to your spouse? YES or NO _____

13. Do you try to overrule your husband's authority as the head of the house?

_____

_____

14. What is submission?

_____

_____

_____

_____

15. What is respect?

_____

_____

_____

_____

16. What are your roles as the wife?

_____

_____

_____

17. What are your roles as the husband?

_____

_____

_____

18. Complete this sentence: I don't _____
because he won't _____

19. Complete this sentence: I don't _____
because she Won't_____

20. What areas are both of you willing to change in your marriage?

_____

_____

_____

_____

PRAYER

For HER

Lord, I come before you to ask you for help in submitting to my husband, help me to love and support him. Help me to adapt to him and recognize his authority in our home. Help me to support his dream and pray for him. Teach me how to be a help meet to my husband and protect is name, honor and integrity.

For HIM

Lord, help me to love my wife as Christ loved the church, help me to protect her honor and dignity. Teach me to put no other human before my spouse and give me the grace to support her every dream. Lord, help me to be the spiritual head in my home, as I lead my wife to draw closer to you and train my children to walk in the way of the Lord. Help me not to be a terrorist in my home or to my children.

Reflections for Him

_____

_____

_____

_____

_____

_____

Reflections for Her

_____

_____

_____

_____

_____

_____

_____

Forgiveness
and Your Marriage
Issues Undiscussed are Issues Unresolved

Forbearing one another, and forgiving one another, if any man have a quarrel against any: even as Christ forgave you, so also do ye. And above all these things put on charity, which is the bond of perfectness. Colossians 3:13-14 (King James Version)

Marriage Check-Up

1. Do you easily forgive? YES or NO _____

2. What does forgive and forget mean to you?

   _____

   _____

   _____

   _____

3. What faults do you find hard to forgive?

   _____

   _____

   _____

4. Complete this statement: I will forgive _____

_____

_____

5. But I will never forgive _____

_____

_____

_____

6. When was the last time you asked for God's forgiveness?

_____

_____

7. Do you believe God has no choice but to forgive you? YES or
   NO_____ Why?_____

_____

_____

8. Have you forgiven yourself of past hurts and mistakes?

_____

_____

_____

9. Is God in control of your marriage? YES or NO _____

10. Do you lay your grievances before Him? YES or NO _____

11. When was the last time you went to bed angry at your spouse?

_____

_____

12. Did you settle your issues before going to bed? YES or
NO_____ Why?_____

_____

_____

13. When was the last time you held on to malice?

_____

_____

_____

14. Who is the first to apologize after an argument or a fight? You or
your spouse _____

15. I get offended easily: YES or NO_____

16. I am always irritated. YES or NO_____

17. My spouse gets upset over the littlest things? YES or NO_____

18. What is one thing you could do to improve your relationship?

_____

_____

19.   What is the biggest cause of your arguments?

_____

_____

_____

_____

_____

PRAYER

You alone can help me to forgive my spouse and myself. Lord, help me to let go of all the issues I have been holding in my heart against my spouse. Help me to stop running to friends and family with issues in my home.

Reflections for Him

_____
_____
_____
_____
_____
_____
_____
_____
_____
_____

Reflections for Her

_____
_____
_____
_____
_____
_____
_____
_____
_____
_____
_____

Divorce Is Not an Option

If You Quit Now, You Might Quit Again

[14]Yet ye say, Wherefore? Because the LorD hath been witness between thee and the wife of thy youth, against whom thou hast dealt treacherously: yet is she thy companion, and the wife of thy covenant. [15]And did not he make one? Yet had he the residue of the spirit. And wherefore one? That he might seek a godly seed. Therefore take heed to your spirit, and let none deal treacherously against the wife of his youth. [16]For the LorD, the God of Israel, saith that he hateth putting away: for one covereth violence with his garment, saith the LorD of hosts: therefore take heed to your spirit, that ye deal not treacherously. Malachi 2:14-16 (King James Version)

Marriage Check-Up

1. Have you thought of getting a divorce?

   _____

   _____

   _____

2. How will your children be affected if you get a divorce?

   _____

_____

_____

_____

3. Are you in this marriage for good? Or you are always looking for the next exit?

_____

_____

_____

_____

4. Do you trust God to preserve your marriage? YES or NO_____ How?_____

_____

_____

_____

_____

5. Are you doing all you can to save your marriage? YES or NO What?_____

_____

_____

6. Is divorce ever an option? YES or NO_____ Why?_____

_____

_____

_____

PRAYER

I turn to you Oh Lord, to help my marriage last and to help us love each other unconditionally. Keep us together and help us to be great examples to the world filled with divorce and separation. Be the glue that binds us together now and always.

Reflections for Him

_____

_____

_____

_____

_____

_____

_____

_____

_____

_____

_____

Reflections for Her

_____

_____

_____

_____

_____

_____

_____

_____

_____

_____

Marital Interruptions and Your Marriage

Friends, Family and Other Third Parties!

Genesis 2:24 (KJV) "Therefore shall a man leave his father and his mother, and shall cleave unto his wife: and they shall be one flesh."

Marriage Check-Up

1. Do you find yourself taking sides with your parents and not your spouse? How?

2. Have you broken the umbilical cord that binds you to your parents? YES or NO

3. How might you break free from that?

4. How often do you call a family meeting on your spouse?

_____

_____

_____

5. How often do you run home or call home to report your spouse?

_____

_____

_____

6. How much authority have you given your family and friends in your marriage? (Some authority, No authority, All the authority)

_____

_____

_____

7. Do you follow Gods command regarding cleaving to your spouse?   YES or NO_____

8. Have you tried taking time to understand your in-laws? YES or NO_____. How? _____

_____

_____

9. Are all in-laws bad? _____
   Why?_____

_____

_____

_____

_____

_____

10. How involved are your friends in your home?

_____

_____

_____

11. How much do you tell your friends about your spouse?

_____

_____

_____

PRAYER

Lord, teach me to love and respect my in-laws. Help me to recognize what advice is godly and which is meant for evil. Help me to recognize that every issue arising from my in-laws is to help teach me patience, love and respect. Father, save me from friends who would want to destroy my home and interfere in my marriage. Help me to bridle my tongue to know how much to share with friends. Lord, release me from any form of co-dependency on my parents, and break the umbilical cord. Give me the ability to forgive any wrongs done towards me by my in-laws.

Reflections for Him

_____

_____

_____

_____

_____

_____

_____

_____

_____

Reflections for Her

_____

_____

_____

_____

_____

_____

_____

Couples Project 4

My Wife's Best Qualities (A-Z)

A: _____

B: _____

C: _____

D: _____

E: _____

F: _____

G: _____

H: _____

I: _____

J: _____

K: _____

L: _____

M: _____

N: _____

O: _____

P: _____

Q: _____

R: _____

S: _____

T: _____

U: _____

V: _____

W: _____

X: _____

Y: _____

Z: _____

My Husband's Best Qualities (A-Z)

A: _____
B: _____
C: _____
D: _____
E: _____
F: _____
G: _____
H: _____
I: _____
J: _____
K: _____
L: _____
M: _____
N: _____
O: _____
P: _____
Q: _____
R: _____
S: _____
T: _____
U: _____
V: _____
W: _____
X: _____
Y: _____
Z: _____

"Share your list with each other and talk about those things that make your spouse so special."

List ten things you love about your wife:

_____

_____

_____

_____

_____

_____

_____

_____

_____

_____

List ten things you love about your husband:

_____

_____

_____

_____

_____

_____

_____

_____

_____

_____

I love you because:

_____

_____

_____

_____

_____

_____

_____

_____

_____

_____

_____

_____

_____

_____

_____

_____

_____

_____

_____

_____

_____

_____

_____

_____

111 ROMANTIC IDEAS TO SHARE WITH YOUR SPOUSE

The strength of your marriage depends on the choices you make to improve it. Unfortunately, many couples have lost the spark they shared before they married and have replaced it with a humdrum routine. Dating and romancing your spouse can change those patterns and be a lot of fun, but will require some hard work. Planning and energy are imperative for making good times happen.

[Below are a number of ideas that could help you in your romantic expression with each other.]

Now—for the ideas! Here they are:

1. Take a bath or shower together.
2. Write the love story of how you met.
3. List your spouse's best qualities in alphabetical order.
4. Place great emphasis on the little changes she makes concerning her appearance.
5. Give your wife a bath and wash her hair.
6. Take a stroll around the block.
7. Take your wife away from the kitchen while she's cooking and "sauté" her with kisses.
8. Bring home foods she loves to eat but won't buy for herself. (Don't do this if she's dieting!)
9. Give each other a back rub.
10. Rent a classic love-story and watch it while cuddling under blankets.
11. Give your spouse a body massage.
12. Stroll around a nearby lake.
13. Sit in front of the fireplace and talk.
14. Read to one another in bed.
15. Turn the lights down during dinner.
16. Make a surprise call to your spouse while you're out of town (in addition to your scheduled calls).

17. Place a love note under his/ her pillow.
18. Write "I Love you" on a piece of paper and stick on his car while he's asleep or before he goes out.
19. Play music in your bedroom.
20. Shave your husband's face.
21. Put his tie on him.
22. Help her put on her necklace, kiss her neck once you are done.
23. Write a poem for your spouse.
24. Run through the sprinklers on a hot day.
25. Remember to look into your spouse's eyes while she tells you about her day.
26. Make up nicknames for each other.
27. Go the extra mile to please your mate.
28. When you're the one who's correct during a discussion, give your spouse a kiss. Focus on your love rather than who's right.
29. Tell your spouse, "I'm glad I married you!"
30. Fulfill one of your spouse's fantasies.
31. Hug your husband from behind and give him a kiss on the back of the neck.
32. Stop in the middle of your busy day and talk to your spouse for 15 minutes.
33. Place your hand on your spouse's leg when you're riding in the car.
34. Ask for an isolated booth in a restaurant.
35. Become your spouse's cheerleader when he/she has had a terrible day.
36. Tell your wife, "I love you because..." (Finish the sentence.)
37. Do something your spouse loves to do, even though it doesn't interest you personally.
38. Write out romantic notes and leave them in places your spouse will find them.
39. While driving, pull over for scenic sights and get out of the car to enjoy God's creation.

40. Write your spouse affirming love letters.
41. Mail your spouse love letters instead of leaving them in the house.
42. Watch the sun come up or go down.
43. Sit on the same side of a restaurant booth.
44. Spontaneously spend the entire day together away from the house.
45. Give your mate a foot massage.
46. Develop a code word for sex that you can use when you're a part of a crowd.
47. Buy your husband or wife a new outfit.
48. Sing a song to your spouse.
49. Write "I love you" in the dust around the house instead of complaining about it.
50. Set up a surprise manicure, hairstyling, or mud bath appointment for your spouse.
51. Read poetry to one another.
52. Make your spouse a greeting card.
53. Go for a midnight dip in a hot tub.
54. Plant a tree together in honor of your marriage.
55. Make heart-shaped pancakes and serve them to your wife in bed.
56. Bring home flowers.
57. Surprise your wife when she's busy by saying, "What can I do to help?"
58. Prior to a "work day" at home, hide gifts for your spouse in places where they'll find them.
59. Feed each other at a restaurant or share the same plate of food
60. Whisper something romantic to your spouse in a crowded room.
61. Have a candlelight picnic in the backyard.
62. Develop a weekly dining spot to meet for lunch.
63. Schedule a lunch date with your spouse.

64. Leave encouraging notes for your spouse that he will find at different times through the week.
65. Write out 50 reasons you're glad to be married to your spouse.
66. Tickle-wrestle in bed.
67. Put an "I Love You!" message in her lunch.
68. Place a rose on her pillow.
69. Set candles above the bed or in the bedroom (carefully!).
70. Serve breakfast in bed.
71. Hide small gifts that your spouse will find throughout the week.
72. Sit and listen carefully to one another.
73. Tuck your wife into bed, read her a goodnight story (or scripture) and kiss her on the forehead.
74. Remember how you used to laugh at things he thought were funny? Do it again.
75. Splash each other.
76. Dance in your candlelit living room.
77. Play a board game by the fire.
78. Reminisce through old photo albums.
79. Go away for the weekend.
80. Rub feet under the table.
81. Sit on his lap even when there's sitting room elsewhere.
82. Surprise your spouse with an ice-cold drink while he/she is working on a hot day.
83. Join him, unexpectedly, in the shower.
84. Mail a love letter to your spouse's place of work.
85. Create a trail through your home with a string or rose petals leading your mate to a gift you have for them.
86. Buy your wife a negligee that you know she'll look great in.
87. Hug often.
88. Leave teasing notes around the house to create an atmosphere of anticipation.
89. Use a tender-touch as you pass one another around the house.

90. Take the phone off the hook, turn off the TV, turn down the lights and kiss on the floor.
91. Put fresh flowers in front of her bathroom sink and write a love note with lipstick on the mirror.
92. Break away from the chaos of the family long enough to share an intimate conversation.
93. Wink and smile at your spouse from across the room.
94. Kiss your spouse's fingers.
95. Celebrate for no reason.
96. Leave a photo of yourself on his dashboard.
97. Give your husband a manicure.
98. Fill your bed with rose petals.
99. Remember something she thinks you've forgotten.
100. Hug for an extended period of time.
101. Do something together to help someone else.
102. Fall asleep holding each other.
103. Tell your wife you will take her anywhere she wants to go.
104. Call your husband during the day and remind him of your love for him.
105. Have a hot bubble-bath ready for her when she comes home from a hard day.
106. Ask your spouse, "What can I do to make you happier?"
107. Buy new satin sheets.
108. Break your after-dinner routine and go sightseeing.
109. Reminisce about your first kiss or your first date.
110. Cook a nice meal and have a romantic candlelight dinner
111. Drop everything and do something for the one you love—right now!

10 QUESTIONS EVERY WOMAN SHOULD ASK HER HUSBAND EVERY YEAR

1. Do you feel I properly understand the goals that God has placed in your heart? How can I help you achieve them?

2. What are some things I can do to regularly show you just how satisfied I am with you as my husband and the leader of my home?

3. Is there anything I am doing or failing to do that seems to send a signal that I do not honor you or your leadership in our home?

4. Is there anything I can change to make our home a place where you feel more satisfied and comfortable?

5. Are there any big dreams in your heart that you have been hesitant to share with me? How can I help you fulfill them?

6. How do you feel we can begin communicating better than we already are?

7. Do you feel that there is anything keeping either one or both of us from God's best in our lives? What should be my part in freeing us from those restraints?

8. Are we where you wanted us to be at this stage in life? How can I help you make that possible within God's guidelines?

9. How do you envision our future together? What can we do together to achieve that goal?

10. What can I do to show you how much I need and trust you?

10 QUESTIONS EVERY MAN SHOULD ASK HER WIFE EVERY YEAR

These are the 10 questions we should ask our wives every year.
Ask, and let her respond. The goal is to know her heart:

1. What could I do to make you feel more loved and cherished? The emphasis is on feeling and not knowing. Think about verbal affirmation of your love. She knows you love her, but does she feel that you love her?

2. How can I best demonstrate my appreciation for you, your ideas and your role as my wife?

3. What could I do to assure you that I hear and understand your heart?

4. What could I do to make you feel absolutely secure? How do you protect your wife? Physically is one way, providing a safe place to live without fear, but how about emotionally, spiritually or even morally? Tom told us a story about a husband who was watching TV and the wife watched him watch TV. The point was, watching a television program is one thing, watching TV (flipping channels looking for stuff) is something else. Can our wives see our moral integrity and the marriage relationship going down for the count?

5. What can I do to ensure that you have confidence and joy in our future direction?

6. What attribute or practice would you like me to develop or improve? Is there something in my life you would prefer I eliminated?

7. What attribute would you like me to help you develop in yourself? How can I help you in the best possible way? How can you be a true partner with your wife?

8. What achievement in my life would bring the greatest joy to your heart?

9. What would indicate to you that I really desire to be more like Christ? Perhaps a deeper prayer life, full commitment to learning the Word of God, sensitivity to sinful activity, elimination of bad habits, friends, practices, a life marked by the Holy Spirit (bearing fruit – Galatians 5:22-23), that Christ is running the show, rather than you.

10. What mutual goal would you like to see us accomplish? Marriage is not about me, it's about us. How can we make the most of our time spent on this earth?

For HER ONLY

Discuss this list with your husband. Ask him to check the ones most meaningful and then arrange them in order of importance to him. Use this list as a basis for learning his views. Your relationship will be strengthened.

1. Respectfully communicate with him.

2. Let him know he's important to you.

3. Purposefully try to understand his feelings—even when you disagree with him.

4. Show interest in his friends, giving him some time with them if they're trust-worthy.

5. Let go of the small stuff. We all have annoying habits and preferences that are different from our spouse's. (Dave Ramsey)

6. Tell him you both love him AND like him.

7. Either show interest in his hobbies or allow him space to participate freely. (Dave Ramsey)

8. Protect his dignity on a daily basis.

9. Be tender with him realizing he has feelings also.

10. Foster an atmosphere of laughter in your home. Look for ways to laugh together.

11. Try not to make sudden major changes without discussion and giving him time to adjust.

12. When you go out on a date together, don't bring up problems—have fun instead.

13. Focus on what he's doing right, instead of focusing so often on the negatives.

14. Show interest in what he feels is important in life.

15. Give him special time with you apart from the children.

16. Recognize that the first few minutes after a spouse comes home often sets the stage for how the rest of the evening will go. So try to make the first few minutes a positive experience. (And then ease into the negative, if it's necessary.)

17. Give him half an hour to unwind after he gets home from work. Your evenings will be much more enjoyable. (Dave Ramsey)

18. Don't allow any family member to treat him disrespectfully. Be the one to defend him to any family member that dishonors his place as your husband.

19. Compliment him often.

20. Be creative when you express your love, both in words and in actions.

21. Talk with him about having specific family goals to work on together each year so you will both feel closer to each other as a marital team.

22. Don't over commit yourself. Leave time for him.

23. Extend God's grace to him and be forgiving when he offends you.

24. Find ways to show him you need him.

25. Give him time to be alone. (This energizes him to reconnect at other times.)

26. Admit your mistakes; don't be afraid to be humble. Peel away your pride.

27. Defend him to those who talk disrespectfully about him. Remember that love protects (1 Corinthians 13:7).

28. Respect his desire to do well—not his performance.

29. Rub his feet or neck, or scratch his back after a hard day.

30. Take time for the two of you to sit and talk calmly (schedule it when necessary).

31. Initiate going out on romantic outings (when he's not tired).

32. Email him when he's at work, telling him how much you love him.

33. Surprise him with a fun gift of some kind that he'd really enjoy.

34. Express how much you appreciate him for working so hard to support the family.

35. Tell him how proud you are of him for who he is (giving him specific reasons).

36. Give advice in a loving way — not in a nagging or belittling way.

37. Help your husband to be the spiritual head at home (without "lording" it over him).

38. Reserve some energy for him so you're not so tired when he wants you sexually.

39. Don't expect him to do projects beyond his natural capabilities.

40. Pray for him to enjoy God's best in life.

41. Take special notice for what he has done for you and the family.

42. Brag about him to other people, both in front of him, and even when he's not there.

43. Share your feelings with him at appropriate times (but keep it brief when he's tired—sometimes men can feel "flooded" by too many words).

44. Tell him 3 things you specifically appreciate about him.

45. Honor him in front of the children (express your differences respectfully in private when necessary).

46. Give him time to unwind for a little while after he comes home from work. Arrange ahead of time to take your "time out," giving him a few minutes with the children.

47. Get up with him, even when he gets up earlier than you want to and pray with him. (Hopefully you can go back to sleep afterwards. If not, it's a sacrifice worth making.)

48. Be his "help-mate" in whatever ways you sense he needs it.

49. Do some shoulder-to-shoulder activities with him (like watching a movie or taking a drive together) without talking. Sometimes men just like to BE with you and not talk.

50. Be a student of his ways so you show your love in ways he best comprehends it.

51. When your husband is in a bad mood give him time to recover. Don't crowd him.

52. Help him to finish his goals, hobbies or education when you see he needs it.

53. Treat him as if God has stamped on his forehead: "Handle With Care."

54. Work to get rid of habits that annoy him.

55. Be kind and thoughtful to his relatives. Don't make him choose between you.

56. Don't compare his relatives with yours in a negative way.

57. Thank him for things he's done around the house. (It means a lot to men).

58. Don't expect credit for all you do for him. Do it as "unto the Lord."

59. Make sure he agrees with everything important that you're planning to do.

60. Do little things for him— let him sleep in, bring him coffee and/or breakfast in bed, etc.

61. Don't belittle his intelligence or be cynical in your words with him.

62. Initiate sex periodically. And respond more often.

63. Sometimes let him enjoy his day off work without having to "work" at home.

64. Get to the point in your discussions. Spare him details unless he wants them.

65. Discover his sexual needs.

66. Surprise him with a 15second kiss when he gets home from work.

67. Wink at him from across the room when you're out at a group function.

68. Give him the benefit of the doubt when he mis-speaks.

69. Don't quarrel over words.

70. Be kind and courteous with him. (Don't be kinder to strangers than to him.)

71. When things go wrong, instead of assessing blame, focus on how to do better.

72. As a kindness, don't say, "I told you so."

73. Try not to argue over money. Peacefully discuss future expenditures instead.

74. Take him out on dates—pre-planning all of the details ahead of time.

75. Hold his hand and snuggle up close to him at times both at home and in public.

76. Praise his good decisions; minimize the bad ones.

77. Tell him you love him more often.

78. Put love notes in his pockets and briefcase.

79. Sit with him while he's watching TV—even if the program doesn't interest you.

80. Don't expect him to read your mind. (Families are spared grief when a husband isn't required to read their wife's mind despite the fact that the wife thinks he should.)

81. Periodically, give him time with his family alone.

82. Check with him before you throw away his papers or things. . (He may view them as more important than you realize.)

83. Work to keep yourself in shape in every way.

84. Let him express himself freely, without fear of being called stupid or illogical.

85. Carefully choose your words. Remember to "speak the truth in LOVE."

86. Don't criticize him in front of others—keeping his dignity intact.

87. Visit his childhood home with him.

88. When you're angry, express it in respectful ways. Don't give him the silent treatment.

89. Pray for him.

90. Make him homemade soup when he's sick.

91. Look your best—dress to honor him and make him proud to be seen with you.

92. Support him when someone tries to put him down. Be his best cheerleader.

93. Don't disagree with him in front of the children.

94. Take him for a weekend get-away without the children.

95. Cheer his successes whether in business or in other areas of everyday living.

96. Graciously teach him how to demonstrate his love for you.

97. Give him coupons to redeem—maybe for a back scratch or a shoulder rub.

98. Buy him a gift certificate to his favorite lunch spot and put it in his wallet.

99. Hide notes for him around the house where only he will find them.

100. Thank him for just being himself.

Notes

FOR HIM ONLY

Discuss this list with your wife. Ask her to check the ones meaningful to her, and then have her tell you the order she considers most important. Use this list to learn what speaks "love" to her. Your relationship can be greatly strengthened by using this as a guideline.

1. Start and/or end each day by holding hands and praying together with your wife.

2. Pray for her every day and make it a point to pray with her when she is troubled.

3. Communicate with her instead of talking AT her or shutting her out emotionally.

4. Talk to her respectfully without demeaning her or hurting her feelings.

5. Compliment her for the giftedness you see in her. Be specific.

6. Show interest in her friends and give her time to be with them.

7. Do something active together to lift her spirit —even taking a walk hand-in-hand.

8. Express to her that you need and value her.

9. Show enthusiasm for the things that she's excited about—let your actions show it.

10. Find something that makes you laugh together.

11. Put your arms around her when she needs comfort, holding her silently.

12. Surprise her by doing something you think she would want done before she asks.

13. Try not to make sudden changes without discussing them with her first.

14. Show interest in that which she values as important in her life.

15. Allow your wife to teach you things without being defensive.

16. When you feel you must correct her, be gentle —speaking the truth in LOVE. Allow her to teach you things without being defensive.

17. Let go of the small stuff. We all have annoying habits and preferences that are different from our spouse's. (Dave Ramsey)

18. Show her that she matters more to you than any activity you could do or any one you could be with that somehow threatens her sense of security in your marriage.

19. Be a good listener. Show her you value what she says.

20. Plan a mini-honeymoon, where the two of you can spend quality time together.

21. Go shopping with her and don't sigh or look at what time it is even once.

22. Take her out to breakfast or make her breakfast (cleaning up afterward).

23. Make time to set specific goals with her to achieve together for each year.

24. Give her grace when she offends you and forgive (even as you want to be forgiven).

25. Find ways to help her know you are her partner in all areas of life.

26. Be polite, courteous and mannerable with her—not taking her for granted.

27. Exhibit humility; admit your mistakes, and ask for forgiveness. She'll appreciate that!

28. Defend her to others—especially to your family.

29. Don't belittle her intelligence.

30. Scratch her back, rub her feet or her rub her neck—whatever she'd prefer.

31. Get up in the middle of the night (let her stay in bed) to take care of your upset child.

32. Be especially helpful when she is not feeling well.

33. When you've been apart for a time and she asks how your day went, don't just say "fine" — actually give her details.

34. Thank God for her by name when the two of you are praying together.

35. Try not to argue over money. Peacefully discuss future expenditures instead.

36. Don't embarrass her by arguing with her in front of others.

37. Lead your family in their spiritual relationship with God. This is important to her.

38. Make eye contact when she is talking to you and when you are talking with her.

39. Show her that you prefer her to others—give her your attention whenever possible.

40. Relate what happened at work or whatever you did apart from her.

41. Stay away from web sites, chat rooms or anything that gives you sexual gratification from anyone other than your wife.

42. Be helpful and cooperative, both before, and during the time you have other people over to your home. (If you're not sure what to do, just say to your wife "What can I do that would help the most?")

43. Brag about her to others, both in front of her and when she is not with you.

44. Surprise her from time-to-time with a card and flowers or a little gift.

45. Remember to tell her or call her as soon as you know you are going to be late.

46. Give her your undivided attention when she wants to talk.

47. Guard your tongue from saying "unwholesome words" or downgrading her.

48. Refuse to compare her unfavorably with others.

49. Encourage her to relax in some way while you clean up after dinner.

50. Be an involved partner and father in helping with the children and spending time together.

51. Maintain good grooming habits so you look and smell good. It shows you care.

52. Be supportive. Help her to finish her education and goals that are important to her.

53. View and treat her as if God put a sign over her that said, "Make me feel special."

54. Run errands without complaining.

55. Give her the love gift of being thoughtful and considerate to her relatives.

56. Don't negatively compare her relatives with yours.

57. Sit close to her —even when you are just watching television.

58. Be verbally supportive and honor her in front of the children.

59. Show her you are her marital partner by not making plans without her knowing and agreeing with them (unless it's a surprise for her).

60. Pro-actively do things that makes her feel cherished as a woman and as a wife.

61. Keep her trust at all costs. Leave no gray area, when it comes to other female relationships, money and your word. (Dave Ramsey)

62. Surprise her by asking her to give you a list of 3 things she'd like done around the house within the next month. And then make it your goal to do them.

63. Ask her and then listen to what makes her fearful and insecure (without judging).

64. Pray about and act upon what you can do to alleviate those fears.

65. Find out what her sexual needs are (and then try to fulfill them).

66. Surprise her with a 15-second kiss (with no expectations to go any further).

67. Keep yourself in as good of shape as is reasonable so she's proud to be with you.

68. Make it a point to write a mission statement together for your marriage and family.

69. Take the time to touch every day—even if it's only for a minute or two.

70. Be polite and kind. (Often we're kinder to strangers than we are to our spouse.)

71. Be sensitive enough to ask her if you offend or hurt her sexually in any way.

72. Go out of your way to help her feel valued over everyone else.

73. Consider her as your marital partner in how you spend money.

74. Continue to court her. You dated her before marriage which helped you to fall in love, now date her to STAY in love.

75. Be careful to choose your words, especially when angry.

76. Show affection for her in front of friends.

77. Make sure your children speak to her and treat her in respectful ways.

78. Make a point of honoring anniversaries, birthdays and other special occasions.

79. Make sure she has money each paycheck to spend any way she would choose.

80. Hold her close and verbally express your love when she is hurt or discouraged.

81. Surprise her by giving her a special gift from time to time.

82. Share the responsibilities around the house (without looking for special recognition).

83. Don't tease and belittle her, saying "I was just joking" when she doesn't find it funny.

84. Allow her to express herself freely, without fear of being called illogical or dumb.

85. Don't forget to hold her hand in public like you used to when you dated her.

86. Don't criticize her in front of others—keeping her dignity intact.

87. Don't focus on the physical features of another woman (because, whether you understand her reasoning or not, that can make your wife feel dishonored).

88. Be sensitive to her needs—looking for ways to bless her.

89. Let her know you want to spend special time with her and the children.

90. Fix dinner for her sometimes.

91. Be sympathetic when she's sick—and help her however you can.

92. Let her sleep in once in a while and you get the children ready for the day.

93. Honor her by not disagreeing with her in front of the children.

94. Don't ignore the small things that bother her and let them build into bigger issues.

95. Surprise her by doing some things around the house that she's wanted done.

96. Tell her (and show her) you love her often.

97. Call, email or text her when you're apart so she knows you are thinking of her.

98. Surprise her by suggesting a marriage seminar or weekend retreat you can attend together to deepen your marital relationship.

99. Express your love and appreciation for her in a love note which you give to her.

100. Show her affection without sexual intentions.

❤ Notes

If you would like to correspond with
Pastor (Mrs.) Modupe Sanusi
in response to her books, and ministry,
contact her by visiting the website:

www.edifyingbooks.com
Email:inquiry@edifyingbooks.com

References

"Twenty-Questions" With Your Partner by Peter Pearson, Ph.D., Co-Founder and Co-Director of The Couples Institute

"Pre-Remarriage Questions: Helping You Start Again" by Bobb and Cheryl Biehl. It is still available through Amazon.com.

Creative Romance... Hundreds of Ways to Say "I Love You" and Much More, by Doug Fields; Harvest House Publishers. Unfortunately, this book is no longer being printed.

Ten Questions Every Woman Should Ask Her Husband Every Year comes from the book Letters to Lovers by Tom and Jeannie Elliff, to encourage wives to ask their husbands these questions every year in order to keep their marriage sharp.